Book of Meditation Techniques

Mike Bhangu

BBP
Copyright 2025

Copyright © 2025 by Mike Bhangu.

This book is licensed and is being offered for your personal enjoyment only. It is prohibited for this book to be re-sold, shared and/or to be given away to other people. If you would like to provide and/or share this book with someone else, please purchase an additional copy. If you did not personally purchase this book for your own personal enjoyment and are reading it, please respect the hard work of this author and purchase a copy for yourself.

All rights reserved. No part of this book may be used or reproduced or transmitted in any manner whatsoever without written permission from the author, except for the inclusion of brief quotations in reviews, articles, and recommendations. Thank you for honoring this.

Published by BB Productions
British Columbia, Canada
thinkingmanmike@gmail.com

Table of Contents

INTRODUCTION

CHAPTER 1: MEDITATION TECHNIQUES

BALL AND LIGHT

CANDLE FLAME MEDITATION

VIBRATION MEDITATION

MOOL MANTRA MEDITATION

AUM MANTRA MEDITATION

HIGHER HELP MEDITATION

BODY MEDITATION

RECHARGE MEDITATION

INNER MUSIC MEDITATION

BREATHING MEDITATIONS

SLOW AGING MEDITATION

THIRD EYE MEDITATION

MEETING THE UNCONSCIOUS MEDITATION

CHAPTER 2: THE MIND'S DUALITY

Introduction

The purpose of the meditation methods within this book is to assist a person achieve a peaceful, calm, focused, and energized state of being. This state of awareness will naturally give the mind and body the opportunity to optimally perform, and entertain faculties that require higher energy to function. This all improves the human experience.

Hi, my name is Mike Bhangu. I've spent over twenty years studying the world theologies and the different spiritual practices. Through this manuscript, I present meditation techniques easy to exercise, and which yield quick results. Try the different techniques within and choose the method or methods that work for you. Practice a minimum of three times daily and for as long as you're able. With practice, you will become capable of meditating for longer and longer periods of time.

Meditation is able to assist a person achieve a peaceful, calm, focused, and energized state because, if performed correctly, meditation frees the time and space of thought from the influences of the body and allows the spirit to influence this metaphysical arena.

An individual's cognitive state can hinder or assist a person reach a meditative state. Every individual suffers from a duality and the two camps are the beautiful half of the mind and the ugly half of the mind. To operate through the beautiful half of the mind, in daily life, facilitates a subtle presence ideal for meditation, and allows an individual to enter a meditative state much easier.

The elements of the beautiful half of the mind develop, house, nurture, and reinforce a value system constituted by such beliefs and wants as the following: contentment, compassion, truth, unconditional love, humility, virtue, righteousness, empathy, etc.

The ugly half the mind is constituted by a value system that develops, houses, nurtures, and reinforces the impulses of lust, anger, attachment, ego (pride), and greed. These impulses hinder the soul from communicating to the time and space of thought.

A common difficulty when meditating is that of the mind wandering. This can be overcome by, while focusing on the given meditation practice, filling the distracting thought bubble(s) with Godly mantras, Godly images, or holy word(s), etc. Better yet, practice concentrating prior to meditating.

Concentration implies controlling the arena where thoughts are constructed so to direct the mind's energy toward one objective. A simple exercise to improve one's ability to concentrate is to focus on a single and simple inanimate object, such as a black circle, taking into account the object's attributes such as color and shape. Initially, keep the mind trained on the object for a minimum of 12 seconds. Zone in on the object. Practice this exercise 3 times daily, increasing the seconds by a few each day, for a minimum of 3 days. After which, replace the object with a simple moving inanimate object and practice focusing on the object for a minimum of 3 days. Finally combine a moving object with a stationary object and focus on this for a minimum of 3 days.

Other considerations that will improve a person's potential to reach a meditative state are correct nutrition and appropriate relations. Now, what is correct and appropriate? That which increases an individual's vibration or nurtures the beautiful half of the mind's duality.

In the 24-hour cycle, certain hours are better for meditation.

Meditate during the early of the night. The Sikh people call this moment, Amrit Vela. The holy people suggest that then is the ideal time because the person isn't exposed to the rays of the Sun. The power of the Sun interferes with a meditative state—it energizes the body's influences. The body must be silenced to achieve a true meditative state. Moreover, the energy the Earth absorbed from the Sun, during the day, is released at night but in a different form, and this energy enhances the practice of prayer and meditation.

> *"Now in the morning, having risen a long while before daylight, He (Jesus) went out and departed to a solitary place; and there He prayed."* — Mark 1:35

> *"When I remember You on my bed, I meditate on You in the night watches."* — Psalm 63:6

> *"My eyes are awake through the night watches, that I may meditate on Your word."* — Psalm 119:148

> *The Immaculate, Sacred Pool of the Guru is overflowing with the waves of the Shabad, radiantly revealed in the early hours before the dawn.* — Sri Guru Granth Sahib Ji, Page 1404

There is a natural chemical in the brain, DMT. DMT enhances a meditative state. Supposedly, DMT accumulates in the brain more during the early hours of Amrit Vela. Moreover, during the early hours, supposedly, the veil between the material and the spiritual realm thin.

Some Christian denominations frown upon meditation, but if *the New Testament* is correct, *Luke 17:21*, and the Kingdom of God is within, a journey through the self is required to find it. Meditation is the only method to travel within the self.

> *"I will meditate on Your precepts, and contemplate Your ways. I will delight myself in Your statutes; I will not forget Your word."* — Psalm 119:15-16

> *"May my meditation be sweet to Him; I will be glad in the Lord."* — Psalm 104:34

The best place to meditate is where the Earth Energy Lines intersect. Most ancient megalithic structures are built where these lines intersect, and for this reason, these sites are considered sacred. The sacredness of a site, or natural formation such as a mountain, is so for the same reason.

Meditation will assist a person garner a peaceful, calm, focused, and energized state. This state improves the human experience. Yet, meditation was not designed to achieve the mentioned, and the mentioned are secondary byproducts of meditation. The foremost purpose of meditation is to enter a state of awareness from which to connect with one's Light Body (inner consciousness) and The Source.

> *"Even the gods long for this human body. So vibrate that human body, and think of serving the Lord. ||1|| Vibrate, and meditate on the Lord of the Universe, and never forget Him. This is the blessed opportunity of this human incarnation."* — Sri Guru Granth Sahib Ji, page1159

You are not your body but the light within. Identify with the light and not the body. The light is the true self.

Herein are 13 meditation techniques:

- *Ball and Light*
- *Candle Flame Meditation*
- *Vibration Meditation*
- *Mool Mantra Meditation*
- *Aum Mantra Meditation*
- *Higher Help Meditation*
- *Body Meditation*
- *Recharge Meditation*
- *Inner Music Meditation*
- *Breathing Meditations*
- *Slow Aging Meditation*
- *Third Eye Meditation*
- *Meeting the Unconscious Meditation*

The purpose of the meditation methods within this book is to assist a person achieve a peaceful, calm, focused, and energized state of being. This awareness naturally gives the mind and body the opportunity to optimally perform, and entertains faculties that require higher energy to function. This all improves the human experience. Good luck.

Chapter 1: Meditation Techniques

Ball and light

This method requests the practitioner to imagine the self as a bubble, and then to visualize a small light that illuminates the entire interior of the bubble. Hold this awareness for as long as possible.

Candle Flame Meditation

This method asks that a person stare at a candle flame, and concentrate on The Source.

Vibration Meditation

This meditation I enjoy. It is the Sikh vibration meditation.

This meditation method uses sounds, four sounds, and four areas of the body. Each of the following sounds should be produced or vibrated in one given area. The four sounds are "WA", "HE", "GU", "RU". Vibrate "WA" in the area of the stomach, "HE" in the chest area, "GU" in the throat area, and "RU" as far up the head as possible.

Waheguru denotes then name of God and translates to Ultimate Teacher.

Each area of vibration contains an energy center and vibrating the four sounds stimulates these centers. While vibrating each sound, with your mind, focus on each area and the corresponding sound. Initially, practice vibrating each sound individually. Then, vibrate one after the other, in a smooth flow. During which, focus your mind toward The Source/The Great Architect/The Father.

The last vibration is the most difficult but achievable, and if this meditation method is correctly practiced, in the area of your Third-Eye, a nirvanic sensation will be experienced.

If you require a visual aid, take a look at the following video titled "Sikh Vibration Meditation".

https://www.facebook.com/watch/?v=1060115440797347

By Mike Bhangu, from the book, Sikhie Secrets.
www.amazon.com/author/mike_bhangu

When the nirvanic state becomes a state easily accessible by the person, the person will gain the ability to move the intense sensation throughout the mind and active specific mental agents, including the 90% of the mind and its agents that supposedly most people don't use. When a person gains that ability, and if The Eternal Commander and Chief "wills" it, he or she will also sense The Light within, feel The Supreme Light pervading, and gain (or be granted access to) absolute spiritual knowledge.

Like building a muscle of the body, to develop the invisible within also takes time and dedication. It isn't easy. However, for some it'll be naturally easier than for others.

For those geared to vibrate, meditate and equate with ease, their potential is greater than those who find it difficult. Just like an individual 7 feet tall and build like an ancient Greek sculpture has a greater potential to excel in sports than an individual 5 feet tall and with the figure of Humpty Dumpty.

I found the above meditation technique to be the most fruitful, in the shortest amount of time than the other techniques I've practiced. To my surprise, it didn't take more than a day or two to experience the results.

On a side-note: It's okay to use this technique and still follow Jesus the Great or any other.

Mool Mantra Meditation

I particularly enjoy the Mool Mantra meditation, and this method requests that a person chant the Mool Mantra 108 times daily. There is no prescribed limit to the number of days an individual must practice this method, or sessions in a day. I've discovered that more one is able to repeat this mantra, the better life experiences become. The Mool Mantra is as follows:

Ik. Onkar. Sat Naam. Kartaa Purakh. Nirbhau. Nirvair. Akaal Moorat. Ajooni Saibhang. Gurprasad. Jap. Aad sach. Jugaad sach. Hai bhee sach. Nanak hose bhee sach.

"**Ik**: There is ONE (Ik) reality, the origin and the source of everything. The creation did not come out of nothing. When there was nothing, there was ONE, Ik.

Onkar: When Ik becomes the creative principal it becomes Onkar. Onkar manifests as visible and invisible phenomenon. The creative principle is not separated from the created—it is present throughout the creation in an unbroken form, 'kaar'.

Sat Naam: The sustaining principle of Ik is Sat Naam, the True Name.

Kartaa Purakh: Ik Onkar is Creator (Purakh) and Doer (Kartaa) of everything.

Nirbhau: That Ik Onkar is devoid of any fear, because there is nothing but itself.

Nirvair: That Ik Onkar is devoid of any enmity, because there is nothing but itself.

Akaal Moorat: That Ik Onkar is beyond Time (Akaal) and yet exists.

Ajooni: That Ik Onkar does not condense and come into any birth. All the phenomenon of birth and death of forms are within it.

Saibhang: That Ik Onkar exists on its own, by its own. It is not caused by anything before it or beyond it.

Gurprasaad: That Ik Onkar expresses itself through God-Manifest, known as Sat Guru (Holy Spirit). Through the Lord's grace and mercy (Prasaad) this happens."
(Source: http://www.sikhiwiki.org/index.php/Mool_Mantar)

Jap: Chant.

Aad Sach: True in the Primal Beginning.

Jugaad Sach: True throughout the different epochs.

Hai Bhee Sach: True here and now.

Nanak Hosee Bhee Sach: Forever true, says Nanak.

While chanting this mantra, focus the sound vibrations near the heart chakra and your awareness toward The Source.

The Mool Mantra was written by Guru Nanak and inspired by God's Spirit. This mantra is a brief description of The Source, and simultaneously, it reveals the nature of the cosmos.

All mantras, prayers, or music written by a truly holy person, through whom God speaks, are so because the holy individual combined specific sounds together to make celestial sentences and these sounds power-up a person's invisible presence. A strong magnetic field is the key to a good life.

A human being has two natures, the physical and the subtle, and the latter can be influenced by sounds and vibrations. Since the physical and the subtle are interrelated, a change in the invisible component of a person naturally influences the physical half of a human.

Everything in existence was first conceptualized by The Great Architect. Then it manifest as a metaphysical thing—spirit—blueprint. After which, the physical evolved from the subtle. Consequently, all material things exist within the parameters of their subtle essence.

Every person, thing, and place emanates a magnetic field, or what some might call an aura, and a person's magnetic field influences his or her thoughts, actions, health, luck, and the type of experiences an individual will attract. The stronger a person's aura the better and the higher degree of positivity he or she will encounter.

The Mool Mantra heightens an individual's invisible presence and this state naturally attracts heightened life experiences. In addition, as with other mantras, the Mool Mantra energizes a practitioner.

If you desire not to practice the Mool Mantra to improve the magnetic field, there are other methods. The simplest, and perhaps the most difficult, is to think and behave in accordance to the better aspects of the human condition such as love, truth, compassion, humility, and contentment. Simultaneously, ignoring the influences of the ugly half of the human such as anger, lust, attachment, selfish ego, and greed. Thinking and behaving as such creates a vibration that naturally attracts success, happiness, and abundance.

Aum Mantra Meditation

As with the Mool Mantra Meditation, the Aum Mantra Meditation too can benefit a person, and for similar reasons.

Vibrate the sound "Aum", sometimes denoted as "Om", about the chest area 108 times daily.

Higher Help Meditation

Open your hands and face the palms upward. Imagine what you believe The Source to be. Imagine light emanating from The Source and shining down on you, and entering through the top of your head. Imagine this light travelling through every inch of the body.

This method can also be utilized for energetic healing, and with palms up and arms out, visualize someone who has show you kindness. Express Gratitude. Then visualize cosmic healing energy (Holy Spirit) entering through head and travelling to the person or thing you visualized (through the arms and hands). After a few moments, move the energy through the body. Apply the hands to pain.

Body Meditation

This technique requests that a person sit or lay down, close the eyes, and focus on the breath. Breath in through the nostrils and exhale through the mouth. Breathe at a natural pace. While concentrating on the breath, take into account how the body feels, and then visualize a loving light engulfing the areas of the body that do not feel comfortable.

Recharge Meditation

Close your eyes and visualize your magnetic field, in which the body is. Then visualize your magnetic field pulling energy from the surrounding air, absorbing that energy, and then transferring that energy to the body.

Inner Music Meditation

Focus behind closed eyes at the middle of the eyebrows. Focus on the light or sparks. Then listen to the sound coming from the light. Listen to the drumbeat, the violin, the flute and discard others. There are many sounds, some are from the material realm. Ride the current of the light and sound.

Breathing Meditations

How an individual inhales and exhales can impact human behavior.

7 breaths in, hold, release, and for 7 times. Keep the mind blank.

The prescribed method to breathe is to inhale through the nostrils and exhale through the mouth.

Repeat while focusing on breath: I will do good deeds, I will use good words, and I will have good thoughts.

Slow Aging Meditation

One hour each day lay with the head pointed to the place of the positive pole. One hour each day lay with the head pointed to the negative pole. While the head is placed to the north, hold the consciousness from the chest to the head. When the head is placed southward, hold thoughts from chest to the feet. If old, the body will freshen. This is the secret known to the masters. This technique is said to realign a person's magnetic presence

Third Eye Meditation

This technique is designed to stimulate the Third Eye and it asks that an individual focus their mind between the eyebrows and push the breath toward the forehead.

Relax the entire self. Focus toward between the eyebrows and become aware of the Third Eye as a small ball of radiating light in all directions. If required, release resistant and unnecessary thoughts, and after which, push the light of your Third Eye throughout your body. Once fully radiating, remember The Source, and request for the guidance to further your meditation to awaken your Third Eye. At this stage, be wise and rely on reason to determine what is real and what is imagination.

Meeting the Unconscious Meditation

Stare into a mirror, into your eyes. Have a candle light on the side. – Face in the mirror begins to change. Faces. 40 minute exercise. Eventually, there will be no face in the mirror. Then close your eyes, and look inside, you will face unconscious..

Chapter 2: The Mind's Duality

The objective is to discover and conquer the dark parts within ourselves. The objective is to reach and evolve.

It's like curing an illness; first, the cause must be dissected. And the cause lies with the five thieves and the five weapons.

The five thieves and the five weapons are units of information within the mind with the potential to influence thoughts. Each unit produces a different awareness of reality.

The five thieves within the mind are: selfish ego, anger, lust, attachment, and greed. The thieves are so for several reasons. They intensify the alienation of the mind from the five weapons and the spirit. They give rise for a person to hurt another. They blind the mind to The Great Architect. And they have a nasty habit of destroying the human condition from within.

The ego represents the belief of the self. Although the substance of the ego is learned, the shell that houses that substance is innate. The selfish ego is centered on the self. Like an island.

Anger is an innate emotional unit of the mind. When the mind is influenced by the mental unit of anger, the mind predominantly turns onto the self. That state of perception naturally limits the information used by the mind's decision-making process.

Lust is an innate ability of the mind and it represents an intense and irrational want. Under the inductions of lust, the mind morphs into an island and is unable to construct thoughts outside the information that constitutes the irrational want.

Attachment is an innate ability of the mind and the term represents a mind unable to let go of a particular external or internal stimulation (memory, belief, or want). An attachment results in the narrowing of a person's awareness and detachment from the stimulant usually causes the mind and body extreme pain and suffering.

Greed is a constructed want and it represents an irrational and unmastered appetite. The term is applicable to the senses as much as it is to an irrational appetite for material objects. Like the others, greed alienates the mind from the power of the collective cognitive condition and all that follows.

> *"Five thieves who live within this body are lust, anger, greed, attachment and ego. They rob us of ambrosia, but the egocentrics do not understand it and no one listens to their cries"* (Guru Amar Das, Sorath)

The five weapons are: love, truth, contentment, compassion and humility.

The Sikh philosophy asks that a person attempt to conquer both the five thieves and the five weapons. When those influences no longer influence the construction of thoughts, a person is able to see reality in its absolute condition. In such a state of awareness, an individual is considered "Jivan Mukti" and the identical self has consumed the self.

To conquer the weapons and the thieves is the objective but that's easier said than done. According to the Sikh philosophy, an individual can't conquer the mind without celestial support.

That said, a person can begin by attempting to subordinate the influences of the five thieves. They are the influences that manifest negative karma and block the influences of love, truth, contentment, humility and compassion. The influences of the five weapons do not have the same destructive impact on an individual's karma. After which, struggle to tame the five weapons.

Books by Mike Bhangu

www.ingramcontent.com/pod-product-compliance
Lightning Source LLC
Chambersburg PA
CBHW050330010526
44119CB00050B/743